Life expectancy would grow by leaps and bounds if green vegetables smelled as good as bacon.
...Doug Larson

IDA GODBOLD

100 Years and Counting!

By

JEAN SHAW

Dedication

This book is dedicated to my Grandma Godbold who will reach her 100th Birthday on17th June, 2014.

It is a brief insight into the life of an extraordinary lady so all her descendents will know what an amazing ancestor they had.

Copyright © 2014 Jean Shaw.

All rights reserved. No portion of this book may be reproduced mechanically, electronically, or by any other means, including photocopying, without written permission of the publisher. It is illegal to copy this book, post it to a website, or distribute it by any other means without permission from the publisher.

Jean Shaw

http://jeanshawbooks.info
http://www.amazon.com/Jean-Shaw/e/B001K8A1A0

Limits of Liability and Disclaimer of Warranty

The author and publisher shall not be liable for your misuse of this material. This book is strictly for informational and educational purposes.

Warning – Disclaimer

The purpose of this book is to educate and entertain. The author and/or publisher shall have neither liability nor responsibility to anyone with respect to any loss or damage caused, or alleged to be caused, directly or indirectly by the information contained in this book.

Table Of Contents

Dedication	iv
Introduction	9
Happy Childhood	11
School Days	14
Working Girl	22
London Calling	26
Harry and Married Life	29
Motherhood	36
Moving House	45
Family Get Togethers	53
Holidays	56
Anniversaries	61
Animals and People	64
Health and Recreation	69
In The Care Home	74
Ida Godbold	83
In Closing	86
Ida and Harry's Family Tree	88
Family Word Searches	90
About the Author	95
Other Books By Jean Shaw	96

A good laugh and a long sleep are the best cures in the doctor's book.
...Irish Proverb

Introduction

It doesn't matter who you talk to, everyone thinks their generation was the best.

Even those who experienced tremendous hardships recall mostly the good bits, and my Grandma is no exception.

Whilst she's survived two world wars and been surrounded by lots of death, endured years of hard work without the modern conveniences we now take for granted, she still maintains she's probably seen the best in mankind.

She's helped bring babies into the world, and washed and lain dead people out, something common for many people of her generation.

She comes from an era when people were strong, resilient and didn't just care about material things, but friends and neighbours too.

They were proud, independent and hard working. They didn't rely on handouts, didn't think the world owed them any favours and when things were broke, they fixed them.

That went for relationships as well as "stuff", and it's a philosophy many of us would do well to adopt.

This is the story of my Grandma Godbold, and is based on the conversations we've had together over the years.

Whilst it will be of most interest to her family, Ida Godbod, is a remarkable woman in my opinion.

She's part of my history. Indeed, but for her I wouldn't be here to tell this tale, so if you're sitting comfortably, let me tell you a little bit about the woman who's top of my family tree.

1
Happy Childhood

On 17th June, 1914, in the summer just before the outbreak of the First World War, Ida Marjory Newell was born at Head Fen, Pymoor.

Jack and Hannah Newell - Ida's parents

She was the youngest daughter of Jack and Hannah Newell, and had one stepbrother called Tom, and four elder sisters named, Ethel, Dorothy (Dot), Alice Amelia (Milly) and Lilian Rose (Rose).

They were a large and close family who made their own entertainment. There was no television or video games in those days, and the children would run and play outside in the fresh air to amuse themselves.

The Newell family were poor but happy.

They had two sets of clothes, one for normal wear and the other for Sunday best, and each week would don their best clothes to attend the three services at the Steam Engine Chapel for Sunday worship.

It meant they had no time to play on the Sabbath, because the children had to set off across the fields for the 11.00 a.m., 3.00 p.m. and 6.00 p.m. meetings, and by the time they got back home, it was almost time to go back again.

Families were large in those days, and all the children from the village and nearby droves attended the same school.

Everyone knew their neighbours and looked out for them.

Doors were left unlocked, children played outside, elders were respected, and everyone mucked in to help each other out if they could.

In many ways it was a much safer and more blissful time to live despite all the hardships, and lack of modern conveniences.

2

School Days

From the age of five years until she left at fourteen, Ida was a pupil at Pymoor School. She was nicknamed "Knowall Newell", but it was just harmless banter, unlike the serious bullying so prevalent in today's society.

Ida didn't take any notice.

Young Ida "Knowall Newell"

The building was originally designed to be used as a school on weekdays and a mission church on Sundays; and at its peak could accommodate a total of 158 children, including infants.

Today it's a private dwelling, but back then Ida would walk the two miles to and from home each day with a group of about fifteen other children, including some of her sisters.

Walking wasn't a problem in those days. Everyone did it and there was no fear of being run over or suffering from traffic pollution as there was only one car in the village.

That automobile belonged to a farmer called Martin Wilkin, but he only used it on Thursdays to go to the market in Ely almost six miles away, so for most of the week the roads were relatively quiet.

There certainly wasn't the congestion, many of us are so familiar with these days, but equally the roads weren't as good.

Few were suitable for automobiles, and those vehicles which did appear were pretty noisy, uncomfortable and had a tendency to frighten the horses, which were a familiar sight on the roads at the time.

Walking was safe and a perfectly normal way to get around, although a few of the more well off people did have bicycles.

If these were left by the side of the road, or propped against a wall or fence, they remained there until the rightful owners returned to collect them.

No-one ever though of stealing them

.

Pymoor School - Ida was in the back row, second from the right.

Lessons began at Pymoor School at 9.00 a.m. and finished at 3.15 p.m. At least they did in winter, but in summer they ended at 3.30 p.m., and if it was foggy, children left school at about 2.00 p.m.

Each of the classes contained forty plus children and there was one teacher for each class. That would be unheard of these days, but back then children had a lot of respect for adults and wouldn't dream of answering back or misbehaving.

There were three classes plus the infants, and if you didn't have any absences in a school year, you received a certificate.

It was something to aim for, but Ida never got one.

The children sat in rows of about eight at long desks, and the lessons were taught to the whole class. Everyone learned the same things.

The teacher wrote on a black board and the children wrote on paper with a pen which they dipped into an ink well.

It was a messy affair, but they were all taught their ABC's and their times tables, which came in really handy when they left school and had to fend for themselves.

There were no calculators when Ida was a child, or any Google to help you out if you wanted to know something.

You had to ask questions, listen, learn and remember.

As she got older the classes mainly consisted of knitting socks for the schoolmaster, or making lace for his wife, who was the infant teacher. She used the lace to sew around the edges of pillowcases.

(The knitting classes served Ida well though, and until her late nineties, Grandma continued to knit bed socks. She must have knitted thousands of pairs in all different colours over the years, and we have several in our family).

There were no school meals and the children took sandwiches. In winter they could buy a cup of hot cocoa for one halfpenny to get warm.

The equivalent of that coin no longer exists, but in Ida's childhood, the UK currency was in pounds, shillings and pence. (£, s, d).

There were 12 pennies to a shilling and 20 shillings to a pound. We still have the pound in 2014, but now it's a coin. In Ida's day it was a note.

Just image, if inflation hadn't set in and she went to her school today with £1, she'd be able to buy 480 cups of hot cocoa.

What a thought!

Another thing you might want to imagine, if you can, is having just one solitary coal filled tortoiseshell stove to heat the entire school. It had big iron railings round it so the children didn't get too close.

Central heating just didn't exist then though, so it's just as well the children were tough as most of the building was pretty cold. They didn't get to go home when the temperature dropped a bit, as is the case these days.

They had to be tough too because punishment for any child who misbehaved was a ruler across the knuckles, or the cane. No soft detentions in those days.

Whilst, many people say the cane was cruel, there are equally as many others who claim respect for rules and society started to deteriorate when it was scrapped.

It was certainly a deterrent and the cane was used for punishment in those days . Whilst Ida was never on the receiving end, her sister Rose felt it once.

You see, the school was close to the river and the children weren't allowed to leave the playground during school times. However, one day a group of them sneaked out one break and went up to the riverbank.

They might have gotten away with it, but as they rolled happily down the slope, Ernie Gray, who was another student in the same class, accidentally caught Rose's face with his hobnail boots.

It meant she went back into the classroom with a black eye, which didn't escape the notice of the teacher. Instead of sympathy, Rose received the cane, and needless to say, she didn't do it again!

Apart from the six weeks in summer, school holidays were short. The children only got half a day for Good Friday, and a short Christmas break.

They were happy times for the most part though, at least until Ida lost her mother to cancer when she was just twelve. It meant she had to grow up fast, and too soon her school days came to an end.

At the tender age of fourteen, Ida left school one Friday afternoon in June, 1928, and started working the following Monday morning.

Her carefree, innocent days of childhood were over.

3
Working Girl

Ida's first job was at the Glazier's Arms in Ely, a pub which used to be on the corner of Broad Street and Fore Hill.

The cathedral city of Ely, used to have a thriving livestock and agricultural market, and was a hub of activity.

It's about six miles from Pymoor, but back in 1928, when there were no real transport links, that was a long way for Ida to travel from the village where she'd grown up. That's why Martin Wilkin liked to use his car on Thursdays!

Ida was employed as a maid and spent many an hour on her hands and knees scrubbing the bars and toilets. However, that job only lasted a short time as her dad Jack needed her to help out on the land.

The name Pymoor means "flies over bog", and if you ever visit the village, you'll see the sign shows a dragonfly sitting on a bullrush in marshland.

The fenland lies below sea level and in the past all the area surrounding Ely including Pymoor had been bogs and marshland. However, over the years the area has been very successfully drained with a network of rivers, drains and ditches.

When Ida was a young girl though, it was a typical agricultural village with local farmers growing many different food types in the rich fen soil.

Jack Newell with his daughters. Ida is again second from the right .

The local farmers grew lots of beet and potatoes. Many used a horse and cart to move their produce, and during the sugarbeet season, Ida soon became proficient in driving the horse and cart to and from the station at Pymoor Siding.

She would take the loaded cart from the fields to the waiting trucks where the beet was emptied, and then return to have it filled again.

Ida liked the horses, but it was a hard life and physically demanding. However, with little machinery around to ease the load, it was one many people endured and were grateful for.

However, change was on the horizon.

Some time before Ida left school, Ethel, her eldest sister had met and married John Baldwin, a construction worker employed to help put the bridge over the Hundred Foot river at Pymoor.

The newly weds had moved to Buckhurst Hill in Essex, but when Ethel came home for Christmas in 1928, Ida who'd left school the previous summer, asked if she could go back with her.

She wanted the chance to improve her life and Ethel agreed.

Jack Newell gave his youngest daughter ten shillings (fifty pence) and his blessing.

He knew a life on the land was no life for one so young, and he trusted his elder daughter to look after her.

So, with that small amount of money, and the few clothes she possessed, Ida set off with her big sister in search of a new life.

4
London Calling

Ethel and John rented two rooms in an old lady's house and Ida was able to join them. She rented a box room in the same establishment for five shillings (twenty five pence) each week.

In order to cover her rent, Ida answered an advertisement in a shop window placed by an elderly couple.

They required a maid to look after them and their large house, and Ida began work immediately.

Her pay was seventeen shillings (eighty five pence) per week, and as the house was two miles from where she lived, Ida bought a return train ticket each day costing one old penny!

The old lady had severe diabetes and Ida was given instructions what to do if she ever went into a coma.

Fortunately she never did.

Whilst the job was much easier than land work, Ida needed more money to survive. Unfortunately the elderly couple were unable to increase her salary, so Ida was forced to apply for another service job.

When she attended the interview, her prospective employer recognised her country accent. It transpired Mr Pate was the brother of Nurse Pate from Little Downham, which is the village next to Pymoor, so he immediately felt they had something in common.

Ida was offered the position, and found the Pate's to be really nice people. They were very religious and before anyone could eat, prayers were said around the breakfast table.

Their daughter was a missionary.

Ida and the other cleaning lady, who was responsible for the washing and ironing, etc. had to wear full uniform – blue dresses, caps and aprons, and her duties were that of general maid.

She was employed from 8.00 a.m. until 6.00 p.m.

The work was hard, as there were no vacuum cleaners in those days , just a brush and dustpan, and also the Pate's had a lot of brass in their house. This included doorknockers and steps, and these had to be cleaned every day.

The Brasso made her hands dirty and smelly, and Ida vowed if she ever got married she'd have no brass in her house!

True to her vow, she never did, unlike my other grandmother who had loads of it!

5

Harry and Married Life

Ida enjoyed her life, but money was tight and entertainment was scarce. You had to make your own, and people would stand by their gates and chat to the neighbours and passers by.

Everyone knew everyone else in the area and every day as Ida stood outside the gate of her boarding house she would see a lad go by to catch his train.

He worked in the greenhouses, where they grew vegetables and flowers.

Ida liked the look of him, but knew he was engaged, so didn't pay him too much attention.

Things changed though when the young man went to visit his fiancé unexpectedly and discovered her with someone else.

He called the engagement off and was once more a free man.

Meanwhile, Ida had made friends with a girl called Violet. She had a boyfriend and both of them were friends of the young man.

One Friday evening when Ida and Violet were walking up the road together this nice young man called out-

"*Would you like to go to Southend tomorrow?*"

Both girls replied "Yes", but infact the question had only been addressed to her friend Violet, who was his friend too.

Harry Godbold, (as his name turned out to be), didn't like to tell Ida she wasn't actually invited, so the next day the three of them went off to the seaside together. There would have been four, but Violet's boyfriend was unable to make it.

Anyway, Harry and Ida hit it off, and the rest, as they say, is history.

Ida told me Harry's surname of Godbold originated because some people came over to England on a ship from somewhere and there was a terrible storm and everyone feared for their lives.

It seems they prayed for safety and when they finally landed on shore the captain said something to the effect of, "Thank **God.** You were all very **bold**".

Some people joined the two words together and adopted Godbold as their names.

My mum (Kath) told me she'd always been told her dad was called Godbold because he'd been a "good boy" when he was small .

Where she got that from I have no idea, but I guess it was one way of explaining why he wasn't called Carter, which was his mum's name. It seems she'd had Harry before she was married, but equally, of course, his father could actually have been named Godbold.

I guess I'll never know, but Harry's mum later married and was always known to my mum and her brothers and sisters as Nan Carter.

However, the marriage this book is interested in is that of Harry and Ida, and the couple were married on 20th December, 1930 at St John's Church in Buckhurst Hill.

Ida wore a brown dress and coat with brown shoes. Although there were no photographs on the day, this was taken later.

Ida and Harry in their wedding outfits

Her 22 carat gold wedding ring came from H. Samuel's and cost one pound, but that price also included six silver teaspoons.

Ida's sister Ethel gave her away as father Jack Newell couldn't afford to travel to the ceremony. Harry's sister Emily was their bridesmaid.

Their honeymoon was spent back in Pymoor.

It was a four-day break over the Christmas period, and when it was over, Harry and Ida went back to Buckhurst Hill and rented an upstairs room in his grandmother's house.

They would probably have stayed with Harry's parents but there was no room. He was the fourth of eight children: Grace, May, Lily, Harry, Ethel, Emily, Wally and Arthur (always known as Pomp), so things were pretty crowded in the Godbold house.

The quarters at grandmother's house were also cramped, but Harry and Ida managed to sleep, cook and produce the first of their seven children there.

Derrick was born at home. It was a common practice in those days, and Harry's mum did most of the work regarding his birth. However, a midwife was always employed for home deliveries at a cost of one guinea (one pound and five pence) each time.

Ida kept her pretty busy over the years, and as she couldn't afford to pay the midwife in one lump sum, she paid her in instalments of sixpence per month. These days that would be two and a half new pence, but as salaries were very low, that was a lot of money.

Ida often felt the instalments would never stop, as with three further home births, she only just managed to pay off one debt before she had to start all over again!

After Derrick's birth, Ida no longer worked, but by then Harry had left his job at the greenhouses and started a five-year apprenticeship as a bricklayer for which he received the princely sum of £2 per week.

This change of occupation served him really well over the years though, and every year since his retirement and long after his death, Ida receives an annual Christmas bonus from one of his previous employers.

He claims Harry was one of the "best bricklayers he'd ever had".

Shortly after the birth of their first son, Harry and Ida moved out of the cramped room in his grandmother's house into two rooms in a house which stood by the side of the railway.

It was noisy, but they had more space.

From there they moved to a downstairs flat in Buckhurst Hill where their first daughter was born. She was christened Kathleen, but everyone knows her as Kath, and she just happens to be my mum.

The new flat had the luxury of a bath, but not the type we're used to today. Instead it had a wooden top covering it, which doubled up as a table during the day.

As there was no running water, if they wanted a bath Harry and Ida had to cart water from the copper in the scullery.

It tested their strength as pails of hot and cold water are heavy, but having a bath was such a luxury for them they didn't mind.

They weren't there long though, because six months later they moved yet again to a house in the less affluent area of Chigwell where they stayed for two further years.

The rent was fifteen shillings and sixpence per week, which equates to seventy-seven and a half pence in today's money.

How times have changed!

6
Motherhood

Harry's parents lived in a little cottage in Chigwell and luckily for their son and his family, they were able to secure a cottage in the same row as theirs.

The two small cottages were overshadowed by huge houses either side in the road, but Ida loved her new abode.

She re-named it Pymoor Cottage and it overlooked the golf course.

At only nine shillings per week it was considerably cheaper than the flat in Buckhurst Hill, and eased the financial problems slightly. Money was still tight though, and Ida had to start work again.

She did whatever she could, washing, cleaning, etc., and earned two shillings and sixpence (twelve and a half pence) each morning for three hours work.

Out of that she paid a woman one shilling (five pence) to look after the children, so she had one shilling and sixpence (seven and a half pence) a day to buy food and survive, in addition to the wages Harry brought home.

Times were tough but everyone was in the same boat.

Ida always said she got paid on Saturday at twelve o'clock and was broke by one o'clock, but she always paid the rent straight away to ensure the family had a roof over their heads.

Since lack of money was always an issue, Ida would often walk three miles to go shopping simply because the prices were cheaper.

She had to be careful and make what little she had go a long way so it became an accepted practice for Ida, her sister Ethel, and friend, (also named Ethel), to get together half way through the week to pool their money.

That way they could buy enough meat and vegetables to make a stew, and since they each had two children by this time, there were several hungry mouths to feed

Often Ida would go without food in order to give more to her family, and she'd tell them she'd eaten earlier so they wouldn't suspect she was really pretty hungry.

These days people fast deliberately as a means of keeping their weight down and for health benefits, but when Ida went without food it was merely a case of mother's love!

It's funny the things that stick in your mind, but one vivid memory Ida still has is of a gypsy woman trying to sell her some pegs during that period in her life. Years ago, you'd often get travelling women knocking on your door with their baskets of lucky pegs, and many people were afraid to refuse to buy them incase they were cursed.

Ida told the gypsy she'd really like some, but with a family, she just had no money for anything other than essentials.

The kind gypsy gave Ida twelve pegs, laid her hand on her shoulder and told her, "Never mind, my dear, the Lord will never send a child without a loaf of bread".

Ida has never forgotten her words, and despite many hardships in her life, they've always been true.

Soon after the visit from the gypsy, Harry finished his apprenticeship. He began work as a qualified builder, his wage increased, and Hazel was born.

Sheila soon followed, but in 1939, when Ida was pregnant with Molly, war broke out and the bombs began to fall on London and the surrounding areas.

Harry wasn't able to fight in the war because he had terribly round shoulders which prevented him from joining the army. Even when he stood up straight, he never really was, but he played a great part in the war effort because his building skills got him assigned to work on the much needed aerodromes.

With the bombs falling on London, everyone had to make sure no lights were showing at night, so Ida and Harry painted all the windows in their London cottage black. It was pretty dark in the day, but they couldn't afford any blackout material.

They had an air raid shelter in their garden, and each night for seven weeks at the beginning of the second war in Ida's young life, the whole family slept there.

One night a bomb actually fell into the garden, and young Hazel was incredibly traumatised by the close encounter. Ida was heavily pregnant at the time, and because of the dangerous situation, the authorities decided she was to be evacuated.

Her children had to leave too, but as a whole family was hard to place, they were to be split up.

Ida was tormented by the idea, so whilst preparing Sunday dinner, she suddenly took matters into her own hands and decided to evacuate them herself.

It was a spur of the moment decision and she simply got on a train with her four children and headed back to Ely.

She'd told no-one of her plans because until that moment she hadn't made any.

Amazingly, when she arrived at Ely station she met George Martin, who was a familiar face. They'd been to school together, and at one time he'd been engaged to Ida's sister Rose.

When Ida told him what she'd done, George offered to take her and the children to her father's house in Pymoor.

You can imagine how surprised and delighted Jack Newell was to see his daughter and grandchildren so unexpectedly, and even more so a few days later, because they arrived on the Sunday and the following Friday, he had another grandchild.

Molly appeared on 27th September, 1939, and was one of the first babies to be born at The Grange Maternity Home in Ely.

Now it's used as office space, but back then it was a safe haven for pregnant mothers.

There wasn't much room in Jack's place for the newly expanded family, as Ida's sister Dorothy (Dot) and her husband George also lived there. However, the over crowding didn't last for too long as Horace Martin kindly let them have a cottage just down the road at Head Fen.

It meant they once more had a family roof over their heads, but none of their own possessions. They were still many miles away in the cottage she'd left so quickly.

Les Kidd, another local Pymoor resident took pity on the family and was kind enough to drive his lorry back up to where the bombs were still falling to collect them.

Amazingly, nothing had been stolen, and everything was still intact. People were much more honest in those days and had respect for other people's belongings.

Ethel, Rose, Dot, Ida and Milly - all grown up and married

With the furniture in place, the cottage in Head Fen was a bit small, so to give the family more room, Kath continued to stay with her grandad Jack, aunt Dot and her uncle George. Originally, they were going to keep Hazel, but she was still traumatised by the bombing and wouldn't leave her mum.

Kath didn't mind though. She'd often spent time with her aunt Dot and uncle George during school holidays even before the war broke out, so was as used to them as they were her.

Living so close to her family, she saw them regularly, but Ida often wondered over the years whether she was right to leave Kath with her elder sister Dot, and whether she'd ever felt abandoned.

My mum says she never did.

Ida's husband Harry came back to Pymoor as often as he could, but work took him to aerodromes all over the country. He had a regular wage though so the family were able to pay the rent, which was most important to Ida.

She's always placed it top of her list of priorities. Her philosophy is if you've a roof over your head and food in your stomach, everything else can wait.

I'm sure there are many people in 2014 who will agree with her.

Anyway, the Second World War ended in 1945. Harry returned home and in the same year Alan was born, followed closely by youngest daughter Jill in 1947

Ida and Harry with their seven young children

That was the year the terrible storms came and much of the low lying Fenland area was troubled with devastating floods and gale force winds.

The chimney pot fell through the Head Fen cottage whilst the children were sleeping, and although fortunately no-one was injured, it meant yet another move for the Godbold family.

7
Moving House

Harry and Ida moved from Head Fen into the village of Pymoor. They rented a house from Mr.Darby in the Main Street.

That house will most probably be remembered for its wild life. Once a snake went through the front door and slithered its way out the back, (perhaps deciding it was too crowded indoors with so many children). Ida killed it on the coal pile with a spade.

On a different occasion as Harry and Ida lay in bed they heard a noise. When they put the light on to see what was making the commotion, they discovered a bat in the bedroom.

Harry never wore pyjama bottoms, only a night shirt, so to protect his hair he pulled this over his head whilst he tried to get rid of the winged creature.

Apparently, he made quite a picture dancing around the room semi naked, but it certainly scared the bat away!

Ida often laughs about it and has a twinkle in her eye as she recalls the image.

The floods that year caused an incredible amount of damage and even with all the labourers working flat out the farmers were late getting their crops in. They needed all the help they could get, so a local farmer who was named Mr. Starling asked Ida if she could help with various tasks normally done by the men.

After all, she'd had previous experience of working on the land, and so successful was the partnership, Ida worked for him from 1957 until she retired.

She wasn't the only woman recruited to help on the land though, and eventually working as a team, Ida, Molly (Ida's daughter), Rene Murfitt, Esther Miller, Rita Palmer and Hazel Saberton, were responsible for much of the land work done in the local area.

They also met up socially.

Entertainment and social events involved the whole community in those days, and most people attended the Memorial Hall.

Whist drives were held on Saturday nights and Ida became a very good card player probably due in part to the practice she had every Friday evening when she, Hazel Saberton and Mrs Chester would walk to Mrs Bell's house for supper and a game of Solo.

Religious services were also held there on Sunday afternoons and evenings, and like most people in those days, the Godbold family attended. They had two different sets of clothes - their weekday ones, which were often hand-me-downs, and their best clothes.

Money was always tight, but apart from a roof over their heads, food in their stomachs, Ida made sure the children had shoes on their feet and clothes on their backs.

Often it meant her own shoes were lined with cardboard, because she couldn't afford to repair or replace them, but no-one knew. As long as she didn't show the soles of her shoes, it was Ida's secret.

Each year there were annual events at the Memorial Hall, and the Godbold girls really looked forward to them because it meant they could have new dresses to wear as they sang or gave a recitation.

Molly, Kathleen, Hazel and Sheila in their new dresses

Isn't it sad how values have changed over the years?

Whilst the family considered themselves very lucky, they really wanted a larger house and for several years Harry and Ida had their name down for a council house.

Most had large rooms and big gardens and eventually they got one at 4,The Common, Pymoor. It was wonderful to have more space.

Life was still hard, and money tight, but life was good and improving all the time.

After the war was over Harry returned to his bricklaying.

He was a good worker and well respected for his skills.

To this day (2014) Ida still receives an annual Christmas gift from Mr Middleton, for whom Harry worked until he retired, because in his words my Grandad was "one of the best workers" he's ever had.

He must have meant it too because although Grandad died in 1992, he'd actually retired in 1975. Obviously his round shoulders weren't a problem in the building trade, and maybe we should all be thankful they kept him out of the army!

Whilst Harry liked living in Pymoor, he found it a bit small and a bit far out, so wanted to move to Little Downham, which was a slightly larger village, closer to the market town of Ely.

Ida somehow heard of a house that was vacant in Little Downham, so she approached the owner, Mrs. Bartle who agreed to rent it to the Godbold's.

The family lived at 85 Main Street until it was eventually pulled down, because the council decided they needed the land on which it was standing to build flats.

Ida, Harry and their family were once more on the move and found themselves re-housed at 39 Lawn Lane, Little Downham. This was another large council house with a long garden, and was to be their home for many years.

That address saw numerous happy and memorable family gatherings, especially at Christmas when all the families would descend on the same day.

I remember how we'd have several different sittings for lunch and tea as there were so many of us. Grandma and her daughters and daughter-in-laws would cook the dinner, whilst all the men went to the pub for the annual family Christmas pint.

By the time they returned, the women and children would have eaten, so the men could eat in peace.

As Harry and Ida got older, and the children left home, they no longer needed such a big place., and wanted to move. It was their decision and nothing to do with the spare room tax applicable these days for council tenants.

The stairs became a bit of a problem especially after Harry had enjoyed a few lunchtime beers, so when a bungalow just up the road at 9 Lawn Lane became available, they requested to move and the council agreed.

It made life easier and more comfortable for the Godbold's. They moved in on the day Ely was in the televised final of the ***It's A Knockout*** competition, so one of the first things to be installed was the television.

Grandma insisted on that because Kath's son Peter was competing in it, and Ida wanted to watch him.

Jill, Hazel, Alan, Ida, Derrick, Molly, Sheila and Kath outside the bungalow at 9 Lawn Lane

After they moved in, the bungalow had some improvements made. Many were because of normal council updates such as the introduction of central heating, double glazed windows, and new kitchen.

However, over the years after Harry died Ida, gradually needed more help to live independently, so it also had a walk in shower, handrails on the doors and security locks fitted.

It was certainly a far cry from some of the accommodation they'd shared in an age when a tin bath was commonly placed in front of the fire on Friday nights so everyone would be clean for the weekend; washing was done with a copper, a scrub board, soap and a mangle; cooking was done on an old black stove; oil lamps and candles provided light, and open fires provided the only form of heating.

Most of the houses she'd lived in had been cold and Ida remembers making peg rugs from old coats, which would double as blankets in the winter.

They would "borrow" strong corn sacks from the farmers, which was used as the backing. Then they'd cut up pieces of material into four-inch strips and hook them through the heavy, rough, material until there was no spare sacking showing.

New peg rugs were made each winter and would be put on the beds for warmth. In the summer, the pretty blanket rugs would grace the floors.

That's recycling!

8
Family Get Togethers

During their life together, Ida and Harry had many big family get togethers, including those Christmas gatherings I mentioned earlier.

On her 60th birthday, Ida held a family party at 39 Lawn Lane and remembers it vividly.

It was a hot afternoon, and her son-in-laws were all playing cards and drinking in the garden, which was very long.

It was part vegetable patch and part lawn surrounded by pretty flowers, which Harry had a talent for growing.

No doubt this was a skill he'd acquired when he'd worked in the green houses as a lad, and because he was so talented and had green fingers, no-one suspected he was lying when in later years he painted his daffodils with cochineal and told everyone it was a new strain he'd developed!

Yes, Ida's husband Harry was a real character and at one time, had turned his long lawn into a putting green by sinking small flower pots into holes he'd carefully dug out of the turf

Anyway, back to the 60th Birthday party and whilst they were playing cards, the men got through a lot of different alcohol in a short period of time. That, combined with the heat led to many of them quickly becoming drunk.

Rather than stagger inside to the toilet, one of Ida's son-in-law's went to relieve himself in the dyke at the bottom of the garden and fell in. The others spotted his predicament and went to help, but as they were all equally inebriated, most of them fell in too.

Not all though. One actually fell into the cold ashes of a fire, which Harry had burnt earlier.

In any event, the card game came to an abrupt end and the cavalry was called in the form of eldest son, Derrick Godbold who was one of the few men still actually sober.

He came to the rescue and used Eddie Stearman's milkvan to drive the drunken men home.

The inebriated males were laid flat on the back of the van normally used to carry crates of milk, and once again it was a case of home doorstep deliveries.

Jill put her husband Alan Harrison on his settee but unluckily for him, he fell off.

Jill left him there.

Derek Hills (Hazel's husband) and Eddie Stearman (Kath's husband) were laid on the floor of Kath's house, and Hazel and Kath kept a night long vigil over their drunken spouses incase they choked.

It was a party to be remembered and is spoken of by many family members to this day, but depending who you speak to, the recollection may not be as favourable!

9
Holidays

Ida and Harry seldom had the money or opportunity to go on holiday. Certainly no-one travelled outside of the country on package tours, because such vacations simply didn't exist.

Holidays away from home were a luxury, but once when they lived in Pymoor, Harry drove a lorry complete with tarpaulin cover to the south end car park at Hunstanton for a break.

Hunstanton is a coastal resort about 45 miles from where they lived, and whilst now it's relatively easy to get to, back then the roads were not as direct and it took much longer to get anywhere.

However, Harry, Ida, Sheila, Molly, Hazel, Jill, Alan, together with Mike and Rose Martin and their two children, Janet and Michael set off on the trip and spent an enjoyable weekend there

All eleven slept in the back of the lorry covered by the tarpaulin, and in order to have a wash, they took bowls, etc. with them.

Going to the beach was a wonderful treat for the children whose normal recreation was playing cricket or rounders in a field opposite Bridge Farm in Pymoor, or swimming in the drain.

It was a memorable experience for them all.

In later life, when they had a bit more money and time on their hands, Ida and Harry were able to enjoy a few holidays away together.

They were particularly fond of Blackpool, which for many years was considered Britain's answer to Las Vegas, though on a much smaller scale.

For three consecutive years they took a bus from Cambridge and headed up north with Mike and Rose Martin. It was certainly a more comfortable way to travel than in the lorry they'd all taken to Hunstanton many years before.

They stayed in the same boarding house and met up with the same people each year – mostly miners from Yorkshire.

Enjoying a well earned holiday break

Another memorable holiday they had was in Minehead when Harry won enough money on his flutter on the horses to pay for another holiday.

He was a keen gambler and had his fair share of wins.

The second holiday was taken in Barry Island, and Ida wasn't impressed. There were too many hills for her liking. One thing you can say about Pymoor, Little Downham and the surrounding areas where she'd lived most of her life is, it's flat!

I remember one year, they also took a train trip down to Cornwall where I was living at the time. Back then British Rail were offering a deal whereby pensioners could travel anywhere in the country for just £1 so they took advantage of it.

I'm glad they did.

It was a nice break for them although it was a long journey and they had to change trains in London.

Thankfully, I had some good friends down there because I had to rely on my friend Celia to show them the sights. You see we only had a two seater MG sports car at the time, and even if Grandad and Grandma had been able to get in, I doubt they'd have ever got out again.

Celia, however, had a Ford Capri so there was plenty of room in her car, and as she was unattached at the time, was pleased to get out and about a bit.

It was actually really nice to visit places we wouldn't normally go to, as most people rarely visit or appreciate the things that are on the doorstep. We take far too much for granted.

10
Anniversaries

Ida and Harry were lucky enough to celebrate both their Golden and Diamond Wedding Anniversaries, and had parties at the Village Hall in Little Downham.

They received a telegram from the Queen for their remarkable achievement, but sadly Harry died in 1992 at the age of 82 years.

They'd been married for 62 years.

Diamond Wedding Anniversary

His death was put down to a stroke and pneumonia and Ida still has the bill for his funeral. She says it was the equivalent of his apprentice bricklayer's salary for nine years!

My grandad Harry is buried in Little Downham cemetery and whilst his grave may not be visited as much as it could be, he's remembered fondly by all who knew him.

11
Animals and People

Ida likes animals and although she would never choose to own one, she has, over the years, been presented with a variety of pets.

Molly rescued a budgie once and brought it home, but sadly it got eaten by the cat.

She must have got her love of animals from her dad Harry, who had a tendency of arriving home with a selection of cats and dogs.

Ida always ended up feeding them, but not all were friendly.

One stray dog was quickly returned to the police station after it penned local resident, Johnny Miles against a fence, and another dog called Toby used to make sure their son Alan didn't get too close to his girlfriend by always sitting between them.

Toby was obviously a ladies dog, and whenever he could smell a bitch on heat, would be off. Once he smashed through a window in search of some fun, and the result was not just a broken window, but so many puppies the bitch's owner threatened to sue Harry and Ida for damages.

Another dog caused Ida a bit of strife too, at least as far as food was concerned.

One day she was working on the land, and was given a cockerel. Ida plucked it in the van on the way home and hung it in the shed overnight, ready to cook the next day.

However, when she got up the next morning, the dog had eaten it. Not surprisingly, Ida came out with a few choice words, and they weren't "Good Dog" either!

Apart from animals, Harry also used to bring his drinking pals home for a meal, and Ida was invariably presented with more mouths to feed than she'd expected.

There was one local eccentric named Walter Lee. He had fallen on hard times, and although he was very well educated, you'd never guess by looking at him.

Walter was an alcoholic and neglected his personal hygiene. He was always in Harry's local pub and his drinking had been his downfall.

One day, during a lunch time drinking session, Harry promised Walter he would take him home for Sunday dinner provided Walter took a bath at his house.

When Walter got undressed, Harry told Walter he needed to take his socks off before he got in the water, but to his surprise, Walter replied he hadn't actually got any on.

His feet were just incredibly dirty!

Harry was a good man with a kind heart, but Ida often wished he'd stop bringing animals and people home.

They all needed feeding and he never gave her any notice, although one animal he brought didn't require feeding at all. It was a wind up dog with a nodding head and after a few drinks, Grandad had thought it would make a fine pet.

Apparently, he got a lead for it and took it on the bus with him, much to the amusement of the other passengers.

Ida enjoyed cooking though and was well known for her filling simple dishes. She learnt her skills from Harry's mum and by watching the cooks in the kitchen whilst she was in service.

Nan Carter who taught Ida to cook

Puddings were the staple diet of her family as they were growing up because Ida wanted to ensure they were never hungry.

Onion rolls, suet puddings and spotty dick were firm family favourites. They were all heavy, stodgy, comfort foods, which filled them up and kept them happy.

Ida doesn't really have a sweet tooth, so it came as a bit of a surprise when in later life she developed slight diabetes.

She loves mature Cheddar cheese and roast beef with Yorkshire pudding, accompanied by horseradish sauce, which she used to make herself.

Sadly, she's no longer able to cook for herself, and her food now has to be puréed, but Ida used to be very ingenous at sometimes cooking an entire meal in one saucepan.

At family get togethers and special occasions, she regularly made flat iced sponges covered with hundreds and thousands, which could be cut up into tasty squares and enjoyed by many.

Ida was also quite well known for her cricket teas when she lived in Pymoor. Each cricket team members would pay a match fee so they could have some refreshments during the game, and together with Mrs Miller, (who was Molly's mother-in-law), the pair put on a spread reputed to be the best in the county.

Certainly there were no complaints at the end of the cricket matches, whether the teams won or lost.

12

Health and Recreation

Until her late nineties, Ida mostly enjoyed good health but there was one occasion when she admits she "got to the gates of Heaven and couldn't get through".

She suffered from appendicitis and pneumonia, and so serious was her condition, daughter Hazel who was on honeymoon at the time was told to come back as the doctors thought Ida was dying.

Thankfully, they were wrong, otherwise this book would not have been written.

Ida obviously survived, and until her late eighties, could be seen riding her push bike in Little Downham, even up the slight hill to the Church.

She never learnt to drive although her son-in-law Derek Hills often offered her free driving lessons.

She doesn't regret it though. There was always someone to take her out, and the bus stopped right outside her bungalow door.

Ida played whist on Monday, Tuesday, Thursday and Saturday evenings whenever possible, at locations in Wardy Hill, Ely, Littleport, Queen Adelaide, Haddenham and Little Downham.

This was made possible because Ron Saberton, the husband of Ida's old potato picking friend Hazel, was also a keen whist player. He kindly acted as chauffeur for her, Peggy Jordan and Bill Cornwall, who all enjoyed the card game.

In addition to her nightly excursions, Ida also went on shopping trips and outings at every opportunity, and once went on a coach trip to Yarmouth with some friends.

It was an early start and Ida asked Mrs Bell, who was another traveller, whether she'd had time for her breakfast. Mrs Bell replied she'd had it before she went to bed incase she was late getting up!

Ida laughed!

After two strokes in 2002, Ida became less physically active, and had to rely more on her walking stick and use of a wheel chair.

That didn't stop her getting out of the house though and her family often complained it was hard to find her in.

Mostly, she could be found at the Day Centre in the village.

On Mondays she played dominoes, whist, scrabble and talked to her companions. On Wednesday afternoons she played bingo, and on Friday she had lunch there.

Ida always spoke as she found, and has been known to express her opinions. She's upset a few people on occasion, but has many friends, and her memory remains as sharp as ever.

Ida had another stroke just before her 99th birthday and no-one expected her to survive. She was admitted to hospital in intensive care and the doctors gave her 12 hours to live.

She says she saw the Angels but once again they wouldn't let her through the gates.

That's twice she's been there, faced death and survived.

One day undoubtedly she'll get to pass through the Heavenly Gates, but not before she celebrates her 100th birthday, I hope.

Ida still has a great love of sport and until she went into a care home spent many a happy hour watching it on Sky.

Often she'd get up in the early hours of the morning to watch a particular event, but she remembers the first tv she had as being a small, black and white, square screened one in a cabinet.

It was bought second hand and sometimes it worked and others, it didn't. Now, she has a flat screened tv in her room and watches many quiz shows, as well as sport.

She particularly likes football and when her son Derrick played for Little Downham, Ida was a regular on the touchline.

Back then, she couldn't afford to buy him the black and yellow strip worn by the team, so ingeniously she cut up some dusters and sewed them together.

It certainly didn't hamper his performance on the pitch.

What a lady!

Now, Ida's an expert on the game, but at her first football match, she complained to the referee that a "bloke up that end has just handled the ball".

It was the goalkeeper!

Ida soon learnt the rules though and became quite vocal if she thought she'd spotted an injustice. Once she was almost banned from the ground for telling the referee off.

They do say mothers can make the worst spectators, and be quite vocal. When son-in-law Peter started to play for Ely City, Ida went to watch him every Saturday afternoon and apparently her voice was often heard from the terraces.

Ida is still an avid Spurs supporter, but Harry was an Arsenal fan. Whenever the two teams met the Godbold's would have a bet on who would win, and observers have said Saturday night with Ida and Harry discussing football was like watching Alf Garnett and his wife in the popular TV sit com, *'Till Death Us Do Part'!*

I can well believe it!

In complete contrast to sport, Ida loves The Proms, Opera and surprisingly, the ballet, which she says it is just so graceful and delicate and a million miles away from the life she's always known.

She'd love to go to see one performed, but sadly it's too late now.

13

In The Care Home

Ida in the care home

Ida has now lost all use of her body below the waist. She has to be hoisted in and out of bed and wears a pad all the time as she can't go to the toilet by herself.

Once in a chair, she can't move and has to be turned in bed every four hours so she doesn't get bed sores.

However, she never complains.

In the care home where Ida now resides, she's a popular figure.

Although she can't move by herself and relies on staff to hoist her in and out of bed, her mind is still active and she's able to do word searches, especially now she's had her cataracts done, and beat her grandsons at dominoes.

She still loves watching quiz shows and answers many of the questions, but no longer watches as much sport as she used to.

She participates in anything that goes on in the home and in true Ida fashion has organised her own 100th birthday party from 2.00p.m. until 5.00p.m.

She wants no flowers or presents, just donations to give to the home so they can organise activities for the residents

That doesn't surprise me at all as over the years she's done a lot for different organisations and charities.

At one stage, she regularly organised coach outings from Little Downham to various places, as well as annual trips to the pantomime in Peterborough. They were extremely popular and families paid weekly to ensure a seat.

She has also raised thousands of pounds for charity over the years by organising whist drives, and I've often been given money to hand over to Highfield Special Needs school, which was where my son Jodi used to go.

He has autism, but the school caters for a variety of special needs, and each year they put on performances for friends and family.

Whenever possible I would take Grandma along to watch them, but she is an emotional woman and cries easily. One day she actually sat next to Ely's Mayor and Mayoress whom she knew, and they had a nice chat together in between the performances.

Ida with the Mayor and Mayoress of Ely

The headmistress always used to come across and thank Ida if she spotted her in the room, but really she prefers not to be recognised for her actions for fear of bursting into tears and "looking a fool".

In 1977 though, during the Queen's Silver Jubilee celebrations, Ida was one of a few chosen to be driven around Little Downham and Pymoor in a vintage car.

She was a local celebrity and deserved her few minutes of fame and recognition.

Ida's also received a red rose from BBC Radio Peterborough for winning the nomination of Best Mum on Mother's Day, and in October, 1997, BBC Radio Cambridge came to her home to conduct a live interview as she'd just received the coveted Golden Scroll.

That was quite a prestigious award of which she's secretly very proud.

Ida likes listening to the radio, and recalls her first one was repossessed when Harry couldn't afford to keep up the hire purchase payments. She later replaced it though with one she bought herself through weekly payment instalments

Grandma is a remarkable woman

Her memories are of hard work, poverty and family. She grew up in a time when life was hard for the majority of people, but everyone did what they could to help each other out.

That characteristic remains and Ida has always been ready to lend a hand if she can.

Her family will vouch for that.

Each child has a cherished memory of their mother and they still love and respect her.

Before her death, Sheila recalled Ida practically delivered both her children Michael and Joanne during her home births before the nurse arrived, and Jill remembers when she was about twelve years old she had arthritis and her mum took her regularly to Addenbrookes hospital in Cambridge.

It was no mean feat as it meant a whole day travelling on the buses and a day's lost wages, which they could ill afford.

Molly's memory is of being a naughty bridesmaid when she was about three and Ida having to take her back to Pymoor on her bike because she refused to get in the car.

Kath remembers her mum helping out with food for her family when there was nothing to eat in the house, and the other children also have wonderful stories to tell about their mother.

It's no wonder someone in the family visits Ida in the care home every single day. She's the only one who gets regular visitors, which is very sad, but a testament to how much she is thought of

Her children love her, her seventeen grandchildren adore her, her thirty-three great-grandchildren appreciate her, and her nine great-great-grandchildren have yet to learn what an incredible ancestor they have.

Hopefully, this book will help.

There's no doubt though, anyone with Ida's genes in their body will turn out just fine.

She did!

Ida has come a long way from the naïve young girl who had no idea how you got babies and thought they came out of your bellybutton.

She blames her large family on the rubber condoms Harry used to wear, as it seems when they were first married, condoms were wash and wear prophylactics you got from the chemist.

She laughs that Harry's kept slipping off!

Ida has loved and cherished each one of her family though and her only regret is she's outlived some of them.

She has grown up and grown wise.

Harry and Ida at someone's wedding

Ida is kind, thoughtful and caring, with a sharp mind and a refreshing honesty. When she smiles her eyes crinkle up and you can't help but smile with her.

Many years ago, I took her for a trip to the seaside and pushed her around in a wheelchair. We were with my mum and dad, and on that day I bought a 100th Birthday card.

Back then it was unusual to get one for that age as few people lived to be one hundred, and I told Grandma she had to live to receive it otherwise I would have wasted my money.

She promised me she would, and I have never known her to break her word, so I fully expect to be able to hand over that card and this book at her party.

Now, of course, many people live to be one hundred and beyond, but as far as I'm concerned no-one can compare to my Grandma Ida Godbold.

She really is TOP of my family tree!

Ida Godbold

If I think about my family tree
Go as far back as I can
Ida Godbold's name is at the top
She's part of who I am

Born in 1914
She's not had an easy life
Seven children – many mouths to feed
She's had problems and faced strife

A tough old bird she worked the land
Faced the elements rain or shine
The heat and cold not stopping her
Hard work she handled fine

Wife to a cockney for sixty plus years
Husband Harry was one of the best
They argued and loved like all couples do
Until Granddad was laid to his rest

But supported by close friends and family
Grandma kept busy, was never at home
With whist drives, bingo and outings
She spent little time on her own

When diabetes became a slight problem
She was supposed to watch what she ate
So daily she cooked a hot dinner
Healthy meat, veg and fruit on her plate.

In early nineties, she had trouble walking
And relied on a frame and a stick
Then a stroke slowed down all her actions
Not her mind though, she's still pretty quick

In a home now, she's dependent on others
And life now will not be the same
But despite being pretty immobile
You never hear Ida complain

Each day her family visit
All amazed how well she appears
Yes Grandma's really a trooper
Seems younger than one hundred years

She's thoughtful, kind and considerate
An inspiration I think you'll agree
She's top of my tree is my Grandma
I'm so proud her genes are in me

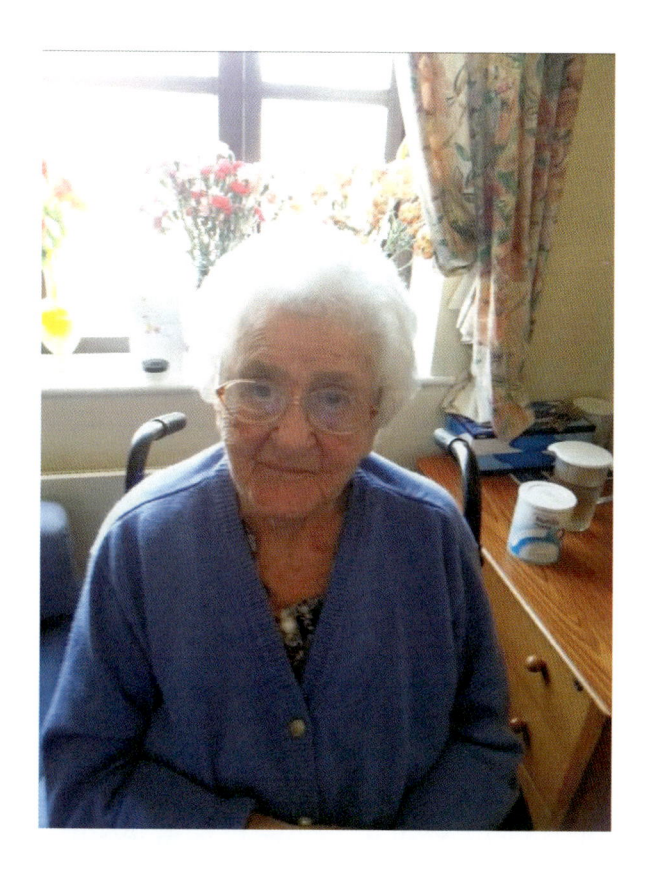

Happy 100th Birthday

In Closing

I hope you've enjoyed learning a bit about my Grandma Godbold. They don't make them like her any more.

I know a handful of widows in their nineties who are similar though and they all have a few things in common.

They've all lost their husbands, but grew up in an age where physical work was the norm, so are used to hard work. None of them rely on modern conveniences and electrical gadgets for everything.

As children they walked and rode their bikes everywhere so built up strong bones and muscles and even today remain active.

They still do as much for themselves as they possibly can. Use them or lose them as the saying goes!

Each of them eat fresh fruit and vegetables and prepare their own homecooked meals made from scratch. They use conventional ovens rather than microwaves, and rarely eat processed food.

Most still get outdoors in the fresh air and grow produce in their own gardens so know what they eat is not laced with modern chemicals.

None of them use computers or mobile phones and they switch the television off at 9.00 p.m. to go to bed.

They rise early, eat a hearty breakfast, and amuse themselves in the day by cooking, cleaning, gardening and keep their minds sharp by reading and doing word searches and crossword puzzles.

None of them drive and if they need shopping, their neighbours help them out and keep an eye on them.

These lovely ladies have rarely ever worn make up, but all have a natural beauty, lovely skins and thick hair which they've never coloured.

Of course they all have aches and pains and their bodies are wearing out, but they treasure each day and take nothing for granted.

They will soon be a lost generation.

My Grandma, like her peers has been resilient, tough, ingenious and determined, and puts her long marriage and life down to the fact she was born in an age where if something was broken, you fixed it, not threw it away.

That's something well worth remembering, don't you agree?

Ida and Harry's Family Tree

Here is the list of my family who've existed because of Ida and Harry. Their names are colour co-ordinated so you can trace the individual family connections

7 CHILDREN

Derrick
Kathleen
Hazel
Sheila
Molly
Alan
Jill

17 GRAND-CHILDREN

Julie, Kim
Peter, Jean, Paula, Lisa
Colin, Suzanne
Michael, Joanne
Keith, Mandy, Shirley
Jochen, Tara
Marcus, Stephen

33 GREAT GRAND-CHILDREN

**Jonathan, Ben,
Kate, Samantha
Iain, Vicki,
Daryl, Jodi,
Nathan, Cavan, Megan,
Rowan, Aaron
Sarah, Kevin,
Lucy, Hannah
Jamie, Tom
Jade,
Martin, Janine,
Harry, Scarlett
Jake, Alice, Molly,
Toni, Billie
George, Henry,
Chelsea, Sara**

9 GREAT-GREAT-GRAND-CHILDREN

**Ella, Carter,
Annie-May
Emma, Georgia,
Kane, Blake, Lucas
Eve**

Family Word Searches

The following word searches contain the names of Ida's family.

The first contains the names of her parents, brother, sisters, husband and children.

The second contains the names of her grand-children and the third, those of her great and great-great-grand-children.

Have fun finding them.

Ida Godbold - 100 Years and Counting!

```
C F X V Z T L A F A R K T M I Y C
R X L T W P L P V N Q K C A J J S
T L D W N A B S P L N F Y S K X J
D A Z A N W R R O K I Q L G M S V
R J L E J B Z S A W D U L G O A Z
V Z W W C Y R R A H A V I I L V R
D F Z W B E U L X O S I M M L N B
W L L C H A N N A H C L T L Y K N
W Q U O K H F R R O S E O L H T E
U A A L I E H S N D O H D I D C E
Y W Y A E X P E V E S T K J G B L
O M M L O T S H Q R D E M R E K H
O O P E F D N O C R A S Q R M I T
T M Q Z B O I Q R I K O J W S D A
I F V A J Q B O G C U E G R V P K
G X A H O G S O D K T H N O N U P
O D A V L E H V O E U X A O Y J H
```

Ida's Immediate Family

Jack	Hannah	Tom	Ethel	Dot
Milly	Rose	Ida	Harry	Derrick
Kathleen	Sheila	Molly	Hazel	Alan
Jill				

~ 91 ~

```
E X J X S H I R L E Y M I C H A E L
Y N G K A G G Y D M M C W T U K R Z
G D B G H Y C M U O W Z M M Q Y V G
P M G Z T S Y K H I D N D E S Q P H
K I M U V T D E X H O C T B A T W J
P J X V B E N I Q J A T P R S C Q A
S W Z E G P A T J S V T A W I B Y O
S X O R P H M H X U I T Z R L Q F F
Q K K H A E M L Z Z F T S R T Q N E
M S Q W U N U B T A T C O T E N X V
D A X P L R V U L N E H M I P N M I
A E R F A B N X U N U M L E F M Z J
Y N F C A S P A T E N U T C O J D W
X N Z H U O L F N K J E G L O K X G
D A N S R S X B F P R S K C U L J X
G O A R B Q D P X R J D H U L J I K
E J E Y E U A M K S H E Q W I F Z N
K K J W P Z Q H O S N V F Y Q Y Y E
```

Grand-Children

Julie	Kim	Peter	Jean	Paula
Lisa	Michael	Joanne	Keith	Mandy
Shirley	Colin	Suzanne	Jochen	Tara
Marcus	Stephen			

Ida Godbold - 100 Years and Counting!

```
S V E H Z H W L X P A E N U Q D I D Z L U C A S F
S C T P H I K C I V C T C F T R B S J W E M D W O
Z Q Z H J O N A T H A N F R J S R A F J C Y I K O
T N A W O R Q A O A F Q V A O A J M D A A L E R X
Q G E O R G I A L J J P K O W R A M R M V V R E F
A L I C E V U B E S L E H S Y A B E V I E U T R A
C A R T E R S O K C R N W A M D W E D E F X Y Q W
H T G U O H E R I L R Z R R N L W O L U P X Z U K
U L I O B I Y M A T L N A A O B J Z R L F K U U P
F L A C N M J C Y R R A H H J I W Y Z G A V C A K
Z C I J A J R Y Q H M Y O J I L N R J V D N Y B L
G D N R T O R A U A R K L V O L B N P C L A G N U
E E Q C H L X Z E N D H C L T I G E D I M C T X C
D B G Q A A Z W M N K U D K O E R H B - S S G S Y
W L C A N A A H J A H M O T O M X G E U A N N W N
I A K C T X Z T N H Y Y L R J F D I X M M I Y R D
I K K F M K N M J O X L G W A B N E M T A T D O G
M E K E V I N V E R R E F E E N N L B O N R C V N
A T T E L R A C S G Z A S T A I G W E N T A J J E
C F M Z L H T I A H A L A R N N M Q R I H M H F N
C Y G N B Y G X B C E N K A J Q J C S N A M D F J
M A D J S Y R H X H C A J W O O N A V A C N J D O
S C T D A Q A A C F T N N X E F C G T S A E L T N
V S Z A S D K M D E Q Q Q F F E T V Y V O T N E I
B C Z W J T E K D H E N A K Q P X E X R C P B E F
```

Great and Great-Great Grand-Children

Ella	Carter	Annie-May	Emma	Georgia	Kane
Blake	Lucas	Eve	Jonathan	Ben	Kate
Samantha	Iain	Vicki	Daryl	Jodi	Nathan
Cavan	Megan	Rowan	Aaron	Jamie	Tom
Jade	Martin	Janine	Harry	Scarlett	Sarah
Kevin	Lucy	Hannah	Jake	Alice	Molly
Toni	Billie	George	Henry	Chelsea	Sara

About the Author

Jean Shaw lives in UK and started writing because of peer pressure.

You can find out more by visiting her author's page on Amazon at

http://www.amazon.com/Jean-Shaw/e/B001K8A1A0

Note from Jean

If you enjoyed this book and would like to leave an honest review at amazon, it would be greatly appreciated.

It really does help my books to be found.

Thankyou

http://www.amazon.co.uk/Ida-Godbold-100-Years-Counting/dp/1499558783

Other Books By Jean Shaw

I'm Not Naughty – I'm Autistic – Jodi's Journey

ISBN-10: 184310105X

Autism-Amalgam-and Me – Jodi's Journey Continues

ISBN-10: 0955773636

Mercury Poisoning - It's Not In Our Heads Anymore – Jodi's Journey Continues

ISBN-10: 0955773628

The GVO Story

ISBN-10: 1466363983

The 7MinuteWorkout Story

ISBN-10: 1470180464

Concerns of Women Over 50

ISBN-10: 1477569847

Jodi Goes To The Zoo (illustrated)

ISBN-10: 1482316250

Jodi Goes To The Zoo (Photo)

ISBN-10: 1493741829

Jodi Visits The Zoo (illustrated)

ISBN-10: 1493741268

Jodi Visits The Zoo (photo)

ISBN-10: 1493741764

Jodi Goes To The Farm (illustrated)

ISBN-10: 1482316315

Jodi Goes To The Farm (Photo)

ISBN-10: 1493741985

Jodi Visits The Farm (illustrated)

ISBN-10: 1493721720

Jodi Visits The Farm (photo)

ISBN-10: 1493741527

A Life In Rhyme - My Story

ISBN-10: 1495465519

A Life In Rhyme - My Family

ISBN-10: 1495492737

A Life In Rhyme - People Poems

ISBN-10: 1495492915

A Life In Rhyme - Life's Observations

ISBN-10: 1495493121

Ida Godbold - 100 Years and Counting

ISBN-10: 1499558783